A JUROR MUST FOLD IN ON HERSELF

Kathleen McClung

Rattle | *Studio City, California* | 2020

Layout and design by Timothy Green

Cover image by Nancy Buffum
"Portrait/Self-Portrait," oil on canvas, 1979
NancyBuffumArt

ISBN: 978-1-931307-45-1

First edition

Rattle Foundation
12411 Ventura Blvd
Studio City, CA 91604
www.rattle.com

The Rattle Foundation is an independent 501(c)3 non-profit, whose mission is to promote the practice of poetry, and which is not affiliated with any other organization. All poems are works of the imagination. While the perceptions and insights are based on the author's experience, no reference to any real person is intended or should be inferred.

Contents

ACKNOWLEDGMENTS

Jet Fuel Review: "The Sequestered Juror Writes a Cento"
Little Patuxent Review: "The Sequestered Juror Writes a Pantoum"
The MacGuffin: "The Quietest" and "The Sequestered Juror Writes
    a Sestina"
Mezzo Cammin: "The Juror's Lament"
Spectrum: "Field Notes, Hall of Justice Parking Lot"
Spillway: "The Forewoman Speaks"

"The Sequestered Juror Writes a Sestina" won the Grand Prize in the 2019 Ina Coolbrith Circle Poetry Contest judged by Andrea Hollander.

I am deeply grateful to *Mezzo Cammin* editor Kim Bridgford (1959-2020) for selecting me as the featured poet for the winter 2019 issue and awarding me the *Mezzo Cammin* scholarship to the 2019 Poetry by the Sea Conference. May her light shine brightly.

Thanks also to members of poetry groups in San Francisco and the East Bay who read and strengthened poems in this collection: Maw Shein Win, Heather Bourbeau, Lynne Barnes, Vince Montague, George Higgins, Chris Cook, Robert Eastwood, Grace Marie Grafton, Ramsay Bell Breslin, Tobey Hiller, Tobey Kaplan, Carol Dorf, and Catherine Freeling.

My Soul-Making Keats colleagues bring me so much joy and inspiration. Special thanks to Eileen Malone, Ellen Woods, Elise Kazanjian, Lyzette Wanzer.

Thank you to Nancy Buffum for her artistry and enduring friendship.

And love and gratitude to my partner Tom McAninley.

A Juror Must Fold in on Herself

For Tom, who listens and speaks his truth
And for all who bend the arc toward justice

Field Notes, Hall of Justice Parking Lot

Already nearly full with Early
Birds, the parking lot on Bryant
comforts me. Bland rituals: square stub on my
dashboard, new numerals each day. Gruff
employee beckoning almost imperceptibly to the
first available space. And, yes, every morning I
glimpse the defendant in his tie arriving on
his bike across the street, locking
it with a gigantic U to the Hall of
Justice rack. The only bike. He may
know I watch him,
linger in my reliable car, CD of
Mozart etudes spinning, spinning.
No contact is permitted—no words or gestures
or notes on yellow sheets ripped from legal
pads. I keep all of my
questions to myself. I am no
renegade juror, will not be
smashing the system this summer.
The judge explained contempt of court to
us. It sounded ominous. I was already spending my
vacation in a crummy swivel chair.
Why prolong the ordeal committing the
extreme offense of asking a cyclist, "How are
you holding up? Have you found a
zone of peace?" I watch him instead, Mozart wailing.

The D.A.'s Opening Statement

Don't put yourself in anybody's shoes.
(The prosecutor looks me in the eye.)
Your logic must prevail here. Win or lose,

this case consists of facts. Do not confuse
them with heart tugging the defense will try.
Don't put yourself in anybody's shoes.

Your task: stay in your own, try not to muse
on how it feels to err and cause someone to die.
Your logic must prevail here. Win or lose,

you twelve must use hard evidence to choose
your verdict. You will hear a mother testify.
Don't put yourself in anybody's shoes—

not hers, not mine, the cops, or the accused.
Go somewhere else behind closed doors to cry.
Your logic must prevail here. You will lose

a lot of sleep, obsess, drink too much booze.
No need to be alarmed or wonder why.
Don't put yourself in anybody's shoes.
Your logic might prevail. But it might lose.

The Public Defender
First Approaches the Box

My client's just like you, except he's not
got gum or ibuprofen in a purse.
His silence is his right. I'll talk a lot

about the night in question, which was caught
on video. Your call: a blessing or a curse.
My client's just like you, except he's not

inclined to ruminate, to dwell on thoughts
of Trump and Pence; he's clear which one is worse.
His silence is his right. I'll talk a lot

about police departments, how they're fraught
with graft, with hotheads prone to pull triggers.
My client's just like you, except he's not

received a fair shake from these guys. You ought
to walk inside his shoes, then write some verse.
His silence is his choice. I'll talk a lot.

Some sentences may leave you cold—some, hot.
My job: to sow a field of doubts through words.
My client's just like you. Except he's not.
He's silent. So are you. But me, I talk a lot.

Superior Court Ghazal

A list of required questions, like an eye chart, hangs over
the lawyers' shoulders. I answer dutifully, can't quite get over

two men in gray suits gazing back at me,
the exact same expression sculpted over

their faces—inquisitive and blank. They're almost twins.
Later each will smile strategically, stroll over

to our box to hammer home some point,
place a hand—cuff link, wristwatch, but no ring—over

the narrow wood railing that pens us in.
The tall prosecutor in particular casts a spell over

me—not the kind on Sinatra records. More like
he probably Googles us, assigns his staff to pore over

our profiles, tailors his closing argument by quoting
novelists we know. Okay, so I may be over-

thinking here, but that's what goes on in our little box.
We can't talk, so we think about everything over

and over—the mother's testimony, the parade of "experts,"
the cops, one with a cane he hooks over

the narrow wood railing that pens him in. And when
the prosecutor takes aim at Goliath—whose shadow looms over

the room—he has my full attention. I almost
grip that slingshot, hear the stone whizz over

our heads. But no. I freeze neutrality on my face, ache
to frown or weep. Later I will. When this trial is over

at last, I will rip that eye chart off the wall,
shred it into confetti, stomp on the pieces over and over.

Notes Not Scribbled in Juror 6's Steno Pad

What is the purpose of a square root?

Alegria needs a new collar.

I can't believe all these high heels.

This trial's like a tunnel.

Pedicure—payday.

RBG earrings—Maeve's graduation.

If I'd gone to law school

I might have a backyard.

Who does he remind me of?

Jim worried about slipping

on the ice outside his courthouse.

I should tip 20%.

This city's like a griddle.

Maybe one of those sky blues.

The Sequestered Juror Writes a Rondeau

You find yourself more grateful for the view
than for the king size mattress because you
don't sleep with any regularity.
Instead you rise and pull the drapes at three
or four a.m. Bright parking lot is nothing new,

and yet configurations change. Those two
Toyotas just arrived. That powder blue
Mercedes left. Praise flux, mobility.
You find your cell

expands beyond four walls by watching who
emerges from each open door and who
departs. One day you will conclude: Guilty
or Not. (Deadlock's a possibility.)
One day you'll leave. For now, here's what you do.
You fill your cell.

The Sequestered Juror Writes a Pantoum

It's no mystery where straight A's come from.
You need a knack for following instructions.
"Sit up. Pay attention. Listen and learn," your mother always said.
The judge said: no talking, no research whatsoever about the trial.

You need a knack for following instructions
and watch documentaries about the solar system, but no news.
The judge said: no talking, no research whatsoever about the trial,
only one juror at a time in the hotel pool,

and watch documentaries about the solar system, but no news.
The mini-bar is off-limits. In fact, for you it's a lunar landscape.
Only one juror at a time in the hotel pool
and forget about those computers in the Business Center.

The mini-bar is off-limits. In fact, for you it's a lunar landscape.
Verdicts don't follow vodka. Vice versa, though, is common
and forget about those computers in the Business Center.
No Googling that lanky prosecutor who doesn't wear a ring.

Verdicts don't follow vodka. Vice versa, though, is common.
Anything goes once this godforsaken trial ends next month.
No Googling that lanky prosecutor who doesn't wear a ring—
until later. But even then, that could open a can of worms.

Anything goes once this godforsaken trial ends next month.
For now a juror must fold in on herself
until later. But even then, that could open a can of worms.
In lieu of sleep or prayer or trance, there is, of course, poetry.

For now a juror must fold in on herself.
It's no mystery where straight A's come from.
In lieu of sleep or prayer or trance, there is, of course, poetry.

The Sequestered Juror Writes a Sestina

Luckily, you knit. You finished the first sleeve yesterday,
wool almost as soft as Alegria's fur, rose red.
No needles allowed in the metal detector. You take
them into court only in your mind. And yarn. Now,
here, your clicking's a jig in this pub of one,
this room overlooking someone's Mercedes, Maine plates, a long

way from home. What distance to a verdict—long
or unbearable? The OJ jury in custody 265 days.
You remember white Ford Bronco, tight black glove. No one
forgets. Then quarters plinked in yellow boxes, and you read
testimony in narrow columns of print every morning. Now
you are forbidden from reading, forbidden from any talk

of this trial. For good measure all your talk,
your mail—monitored. A deputy sits in the long
corridor, plays video games, his "yessssss!" audible every now
and then. You have begun counting nights and days
the way you count cars (eight blue, three red,
six silver) or words per line (nine, plus one

extra here and there.) You see yourself as someone
who'll be a champion deliberator, someone who will take
her time, weigh evidence on a sturdy scale, reread
notes in her steno pad aloud, only humor long-
winded men for a little while, not all day.
But you're nowhere near that conference table yet. Now

you have an armada of pillows, coffee from pods. Now
you knit a sleeve, remember the Dream Team won,
OJ went free. Imagine the twelve that October Monday,
imagine their exhaustion, their bursting like volcanos to talk
at last, lift their voices again after so long.
Did they get drunk after their verdict was read,

[. . .]

did they leave car keys with valets in red
jackets, dance like dervishes, spinning in dark nightclubs now
defunct, or did they instead embark on impossibly long
hikes in the San Gabriels, looking for the one
sacred hawk or wolf or moth that would take
everything, carry everything away? You finished a sleeve yesterday,

a small one, rose red, for a newborn. More
must take shape from your long skeins, your clicks,
from these sequestered days you are counting, counting now.

The Sequestered Juror Writes a Cento

Lines from Martín Espada and Rebecca Foust

There are no words in our language to say this.
They call it being in shock, this state
where gas stations snap their lights off one by one
and we're marooned here now, left
deep in the well where anesthesia
is carnival. From the dolor
blood drums behind my ears,
all of it whispering—go ahead—go
where the dead stand in the rain
soft, and off-camera. Silence. Silence and ash.

On the beach I found the skeleton of a blowfish
and no science, god, or creed
to keep vigil over the waves,
and so I took my place in the line
waiting for the alchemy of dust
and spent light. Sometimes a song rings out
as if the words were missing teeth
made from recycled rubber. I like
my comrade the angry bald man.
His eyes are blue, too. He tells us

about veterans who drench themselves in liquor
north of the old shuttered silk mill.
He lights a cigarette for those who would see the ruins
through a chink in a cellar wall, the attic air
dissolved in smoke. There was silence
folded, refolded in the same locked drawer.
You will not hear this, even after the war is over.
You pack your new purse with lipstick, and mace,
a poem useful as a coat to a coughing man,
the plume somewhere behind him, the fire.

The Juror's Lament

1. *Box*

We must not: speak, return to scene of crime,
(bleak dive-bar street) or, worse, research online
the cast of players in this cheerless room—
plump, sneakered judge instructing us, "Assume
no guilt for now" (she looks like Gertrude Stein);

stern prosecutor, watchful like a mime;
public defender, sleek in Calvin Klein;
accused at table silent as a tomb.
We must not speak,

but pay fifteen to park, arrive at nine,
inch through antique metal detector line
and take our seats inside this box, resume
our stony faces, doused in dull perfume
of civic duty, steno pads. Confined,
we must not speak.

2. *Locked Hallway*

A smaller room awaits us twelve who word-
lessly observed from swivel chairs. We heard
this case: murky surveillance video,
paid expert witnesses who swore they know
who did it, how, and why. So much has blurred

these weeks within our box. We have endured
the bloody photographs, the vague, absurd
insinuations. Now it's time to go:
a smaller room

will house our conversation long deferred
while lawyers spun their tales of what occurred
in winter, 8:03, four years ago.
We shuffle down a hall, reluctant row
of citizens. If we convict, he is assured
a smaller room.

[…]

3. *Verdict*

I print *Guilty* with ballpoint pen and sign
my name. Below I add the date and time
(from Melvin's phone): 11:43.
We've made our peace. We wrestled mightily
for days, the bailiff locking us at nine,

the grim defendant on hall bench—assigned
or self-imposed vigil as anodyne?
His presence brought us no tranquility.
I print *Guilty*,

relieved to finish, stand and leave behind
the awful pad marked JUROR 6, blue lines
thin horizontal bars—a penitentiary.
Success: our reaching unanimity?
Perhaps. The punishment, our judge defines.
I print *Guilty*.

The Forewoman Speaks

Among us twelve, just three have raised a child.
We're mostly gray and promise to be fair
and wonder if the prosecutor smiled
to greet or warn, or both. We go nowhere
for weeks. We're stiff and silent in these rows,
our faces stony though we ache to cry,
delete that damn surveillance video
(Exhibit A) that shows a girl, six, die,
night, crosswalk, SUV. And in the end,
our verdict signed and dated, read aloud,
we will resume routine—go meet a friend
for lunch on Harrison, admire a cloud
above the bridge, ten thousand cars an hour,
some backseats full of kids.

The Quietest

The quietest, he sat apart from us
eleven wrangling long paragraphs
of guilt or innocence. I wondered was
this man that student in the back who laughs
at random intervals, evades a teacher's gaze,
and doodles skulls? We were a jury not
a class that endless week, those August days
we scrutinized dim video and thought
out loud about our negligence, our pure dumb luck
behind the wheel: we hadn't killed a child.
But one had bled to death, and we were stuck
inside that bolted room, unreconciled
and tense. At last the quietest cut through
our fog. A sort of Solomon, he knew

our fog. A sort of Solomon, he knew.
So when he—*sotto voce*—spoke, we fell
silent. Enough of scribbled notes on blue-
lined steno pads. Enough of almost yell-
ing, weeping, sword fighting. We could agree
at last, go home, begin to sleep at night
again, peel back thick layers of secrecy
we'd worn all through this trial. I thought I might
bump into one or two. Our city's small,
ripe for coincidence. Last week nearby,
a crowded diner, loud hole-in-the-wall,
I elbowed Tom: "Look. There's the jury guy."
Quick nods. Rueful hellos. But we did not discuss.
The quietest, he sat apart from us.

Behind the Wheel

Our monthly ritual: he'd ask about my cat,
uncork a bottle, pour us each some wine,
merlot. I'd curse the traffic on the drive—
I-80 East. My father wasn't bored.
He'd nod, say: Never tailgate. Stay safe.
Rotate your tires and change your oil. He'd ask

about my 401, my landlord, ask
what did the vet advise about old cats'
hairballs? He'd show me articles he'd saved,
websites and blogs he liked. He poured more wine
and reminisced: two terms on the school board,
his office, business trips. Sometimes we'd drive

to Jackson, play poker machines, then drive
back from the hills, still talking poker as
the sun sank, blue lights bloomed on his dashboard,
and twilight blurred the road. He swerved for cats
and, once, some wild turkeys, their feathers wine-
colored, their strutting slow. He kept them safe.

A cop arrested him one night: unsafe,
erratic weaving in a lane while driv-
ing home from chess at Duffy's bar, more wine
than usual, more checkmates too. I never asked
how many games he lost—too delicate
a point to probe. My father liked the board

at Duffy's in the back below the old dartboard
that no one used. A quiet tavern, safe—
no brawls, just chess and fondness for a cat
named Stub who slept between the kegs. The drive
from Duffy's—eight quick blocks. He didn't ask
to call a cab. He dozed in jail and paid the fines,

[...]

apologized in court. The judge liked wine
and chess as well perhaps: she wasn't bored
or cruel, just firm, assigning Dad the task
of office help, SPCA. They saved
a few, he told me, their spring Kitten Drive
a big success. He typed cage cards for cats

and dogs newly arrived. His fingers swift
on sleek keyboard, he saved to the hard drive:
Old cats are like fine wines. Ask any volunteer.

Summons

for Ellen Marguerite Park Henderson, 1901–1974,
who gave me my middle name

1.

She tended roses near her bungalow.
I conjure velvet reds, sweet scent of pinks.
Bee's Knees perhaps her favorite yellow.
Confess: I'm guessing, spinning wishful thinking into verse as memory evaporates.
And yet enough remains for crafting here:
some petals vivid from the past, some gates
still open for intrepid sonneteers
who seek—what? kin? coherence? roots of trees?
Dear grandmother whose name I share, allow
me to weave fact with wish, weave legalese
with metaphor, stray wisps of why and how.
We share at least two syllables. My guess—
there's more to find, both guilt and innocence.

[…]

2.

There's much to find, both guilt and innocence,
in each divorce. When hers was finalized
she went to work full-time, dropped twenty cents
into the fare box on the bus, surprised
herself—her typing lightning fast, correct.
She seldom used the small eraser wheel,
the brush, but kept it in a drawer. She checked
for sticky keys, for ribbon jams on reels.
Each Underwood a personality
with quirks she understood, forgave. Each night
her daughter talked of Civics, Drama, Glee
Club, boys. Who cooked? Did Mom and Grandma fight
about exhaustion, loneliness and sex
in 1948, what would come next?

3.

In 1948 what would come next
was daughter leaving home to go to school
up north and mother staying, static, fixed.
It's here I lose the narrative, the jewel.
I must invent, Ellen. Please smile on lines
that place you in the courthouse, second floor,
transcribing—what? Vast unpaid traffic fines?
Staid juries' verdicts sentencing the poor
to penitentiaries? You typed all day.
And ate lunch—where? A picnic table in
a smoggy park? Was smog still years away?
They called you Marge at work, admired the pin
you wore—a rose bouquet, six faux teardrop
rubies, a daughter's gift. Did fighting stop?

[...]

4.

Rubies. A daughter's gifted. Fighting stops
when California cleaves in two, when phones
in booths need clinking coins and envelopes
need stamps. Perhaps you both chose cheerful tones.
Were you left-handed too, your script compact
like hers? I don't know what or how you wrote,
how far a walk to your mailbox—a fact
that matters suddenly as I devote
my pen to shaping you. I wonder, too,
whether you penned or typed those letters then,
stayed late at your machine, greeted the crew
of janitors, calm, phased-by-nothing men.
I'm phased by everything. What stumps me now:
which words did you compose, Ellen, and how?

5.

Which words did you compose, Ellen? And how
did you make peace with middle age? I draw
a blank. One guess—a small TV, a show
that made you laugh: *Can You Top This?* Dinah
Shore. Perry Como. Probably the news
at ten, which never made you laugh, of course.
Both Mom and I have muttered in our sleep. Did you?
Did you take home the petty crimes or, worse,
the felonies your fingers touched each day?
I ask you, Ellen, now, as I seek peace,
a juror sworn to silence on this case,
this endless trial—victims and police
and video, an endless loop of loss
we twelve appraise alone. Grave calculus.

[...]

6.

We twelve appraise alone. Grave calculus
we each perform in separate swivel chairs,
our courthouse miles and years—some sixty plus—
away from yours. I climb the somber stairs.
Brief refuge in the Ladies room, brief glance
at self above the sink. My mantra: *Wise.*
Be wise. Unhurrying, I dry my hands
to grip the pen, the steno pad. My eyes
will sweep that spartan room, the men in suits,
the listless flag. We'll trade twelve wry hellos,
then hunker down to silent civic du-
ty. Yes, confess: I'm flattered lawyers chose
this thinker striving (mostly) to be fair.
And yet my heart, my heart. Beyond repair?

7.

And yet my heart. My heart beyond repair—
hyperbole I'm fairly sure as I complete
this crown, this summoning of name we share.
Marge punched the clock, but Ellen Marguerite
was kind to jurors in the hall, the Ladies room,
those lingering at sinks, those lost in thought
of guilt and innocence. One spied a bloom
of rubies (faux) on blouse, asked where she bought
her sparkling gems. My wish: she'd smile, she'd say,
"A birthday gift. My daughter's sweet surprise."
The juror murmured words, drifted away.
What Ellen heard had sounded like, "Be wise,"
so when the courthouse closed, she'd catch her bus, she'd go
and tend her roses near her bungalow.

Advice for the Ghost Ship Jurors

*On December 2, 2016, at 11:20 p.m. PST a fire broke
out in a former warehouse in Oakland that had been
converted into an artist collective with living spaces
known as Ghost Ship. The fire killed 36 people.*

1.

Fill the birdfeeder in your backyard.
Invest in high-end black oil sunflower seeds.
If you have no backyard—and who does?—
stand still for a long time among Canadian geese
roaming grass near Lake Merritt. Later, doodle
your favorites next to the notes in your steno pad.
Be aware all pads will be confiscated
at the end of the trial, so don't get attached.
Draw dozens of birds anyway. Give them names.
And just think of them as flying away
when your steno pad is destroyed
by a court clerk after the verdict.
I think they shred them, wire and all,
but you might double check.

2.

Shake sand out of your shoes for a long time.
There's always more in there than you think.
Clap them together if the asphalt isn't too hot.
At Ocean Beach that shouldn't be a problem.
Just look at all the barefoot surfers coming
and going with their waxed boards.
Feel free to doodle these surfers as well—
those who stay upright wave after wave
and those who keep falling
into cold water and tasting the salt.
They already have names, of course,
but make up new ones if you find that helpful.
Mine all had three syllables.
Fiona. Timothy. Elijah. Genevieve.

ABOUT THE RATTLE CHAPBOOK SERIES

The Rattle Chapbook Series publishes and distributes a chapbook to all of *Rattle*'s print subscribers along with each quarterly issue of the magazine. Most selections are made through the annual Rattle Chapbook Prize competition (deadline: January 15th). For more information, and to order other chapbooks from the series, visit our website.